ADHD Child's Handbook for Parents

A Helpful Guide for Parents to Control Anxiety, Stress and Bring Confidence and Calmness to A Child's Life.

AF704842

By

Aiden Moseley

Deluxe Reads

About the Author

Aiden Moseley is a social activist and behavior specialist. He is a professional therapist and mainly focuses his energy on creating techniques and therapies that could help people of all ages. Aiden Moseley believes in creating a healthy environment that could be beneficial for everyone. He is currently working in an NGO that deals in providing mental and emotional therapies for kids and adults both. The different books he has written provides guidelines and effective therapies for its readers and he ensures they get the solution to their problem through the information they provide.

Table of contents

Introduction

"His school's principal called." Jack's mother said in utter dismay, holding the phone in her hand.
"He threw a tantrum again, this time, followed by crying outbursts during the class," she said.
"Our child is getting unapproachable day by day," responded Jack's father.

Jack is a 7-year-old first-grader who has displayed various ADHD symptoms. He has had various incidents of crying outbursts, hitting, and inappropriate behavior both in and outside the home. There have even been situations when Jack indulged in intense anger episodes in public. It is getting challenging for Jack's parents. They are concerned that if Jack's condition prevails, it will also have adverse effects on other siblings younger than Jack. However, the parents are now looking for behavioral therapy for Jack.

Behavioral changes in children can sometimes be more than just mood swings. Sometimes, behavioral change can signify a serious nerve illness like AHDH. Attention Deficit Hyperactivity Disorder is one of the most frequent neurobehavioral disorders affecting children aged 6 to 17.

ADHD is the 3rd most common mental health disorder globally, after depression and anxiety. It affects 3.4 percent of children and adolescents. The development of this condition occurs at a young age, with few symptoms that are typically seen as a natural part of growing up. However, as time passes, the mood swings become more noticeable and tougher to regulate. As indicated in Jack's example, crying and anger outbursts, inattention, and impulsivity are all symptoms of ADHD.

Children and adolescents with ADHD have a difficult time throughout their formative years. They often do poorly in academics, receive lower marks, and are more likely to be struck off from school due to their impulsive conduct and slower information processing pace. Impulsivity also raises the likelihood of car accidents and spontaneous sexual hassles, explaining why youngsters with ADHD have more teen pregnancies and are more likely to contract sexually transmitted illnesses. Low self-esteem is also part of ADHD-related problems.

There are instances when an ADHD kid is misunderstood by parents and other fellows if there is a lack of awareness about the matter. Such a further approach adds to the problem. Therefore, parents and caregivers should understand their child's ADHD symptoms and need greater attention and respond accordingly.

Parents should accept that ADHD only indicates functional differences in the brain. ADHD does not imply that a child is not capable of learning. Instead, such children learn differently. Therefore, parents need to look for various ways to assist their children in developing positive behavior. Parents need to adjust their ways of interacting with their ADHD child. Adaptations may be required in speech, physical environment, gestures, and the emotional language parents use with their children.

Consuming the right kind of nutrition can also help limit the unfavorable consequences of ADHD. Children with ADHD should avoid consuming sugars and processed carbs. That means saying "No" to frozen waffles, jelly, and pancakes. Studies show that children who had low glycemic index foods in breakfast displayed better memory, functioning, and attention than those who ate high sugar, processed meals.

Other natural remedies such as frequent exercise, better sleep patterns, and more use of essential oils may also work well for ADHD kids.

While it may be challenging to raise ADHD children, this book comes to save parents and caregivers from unnecessary trouble. This guidebook will assist parents in recognizing the signs and symptoms of ADHD and the underlying reasons. It will also provide a positive approach to ADHD management and treatment. Parents will be able to manage their children's mood swings and ADHD-related problems after gaining an understanding of the book's perspective.

This book aims to assist parents with:

- Developing a better understanding of ADHD
- Knowing the symptoms and diagnosis of ADHD
- Managing and treating ADHD
- Coping with related disorders
- Manifestation of the patient's potential for a better future

The first step to fighting ADHD is to know more about its roots. So, let us jump to the first chapter to know more about ADHD. The chapter highlights some major classifications of ADHD, its symptoms, and clinical features. I am positive the chapter will help you discover the facts you are looking for. Happy Reading!

Part 1:

Chapter 1: Explanation of ADHD

Sarah is an 8-year-old second-grader. Lately, her parents have been concerned about her lack of interest in academics. Although Sarah does well in her piano lessons, she has poor academic performance. According to her teacher, Sarah often indulges in quarrels with other class fellows.

"She is quite talkative during class. She just attempts to get away from the lessons. And she cannot sit still. This kid has a mind of her own. She lives in her own world!"

These were Sarah's teacher's remarks in the recent Parent-Teacher Meeting at school.

Do you think Sarah's behavior is normal as compared to the children of her age, or is it because of other underlying conditions?

It is common for children to face difficulty paying attention and behaving appropriately at some point in their lives. However, children with ADHD do not usually do away with such behaviors. The symptoms in ADHD children, as indicated in Sarah's case, persist and can be intense, causing problems at home, school, and with friends.

Determining whether a child possesses ADHD is a multi-step process. There is no one test for diagnosing ADHD and other related issues. Problems such as depression and anxiety, sleep issues, and certain forms of learning difficulties might share symptoms of ADHD.

The upcoming sub-headings of this chapter will focus on the definition, symptoms, major types, and various clinical characteristics of ADHD.

1.1 What is ADHD?

ADHD is a common neurodevelopmental disease among children. It is usually displayed in the early years of childhood and continues in adulthood. Children having ADHD struggle with paying attention, managing impulsive behaviors (acting without realizing the consequences), or being immensely active.

Hence, Attention Deficit Hyperactivity Disorder is a condition that indicates (inattention) lack of attention, (hyperactivity) an incapability to remain quiet and motionless, and (impulsivity) adverse impulse control. Some persons with ADHD may only have issues with either inattention or impulsivity and hyperactivity, but the majority have issues with all three.

The typical behaviors of children and adults with ADHD are intense and frequent enough to hinder the daily tasks such as employment, school, and interpersonal interactions. People having inattention disorder are forgetful, easily distracted and avoid work that demands continuous attention, have trouble organizing chores, and often lose items as a result of their failure to stay focused on tasks.

Frequent movement is a sign of hyperactivity. When seated, people with this trait usually tap their foot, fidget, get up from their seat if it is unacceptable to remain seated for long (for example, in a classroom), or chat excessively and bother others.

Impulsivity can lead to hasty and spontaneous decisions with little regard for the repercussions. Individuals who have weak impulse control often struggle to wait for their turn and let others do things first or think things through before acting.

1.2 Classification of ADHD

There are three major classifications of ADHD. A set of behavioral symptoms distinguishes each type from one another.

The three principal types of ADHD are:

- Hyperactive or Impulsive ADHD
- Inattentive or Distractible ADHD

- Combined ADHD

1. Hyperactive or Impulsive Type ADHD

People with hyperactive ADHD feel compelled to move constantly. They fidget, squirm, and fight to stay seated on a regular basis. Children frequently act as if they are "powered by a motor" and run around a lot. People of various ages may talk nonstop, interrupt others, blur out replies, and lack self-control. Children and men are more likely to be diagnosed with this kind of ADHD.

2. Inattentive Type ADHD

People with inattentive ADHD type make careless mistakes. They have trouble sustaining concentration, following specific directions, and coordinating tasks and activities. They have a poor working memory, are quickly distracted by outside stimuli, and they frequently misplace items. Adults and females are more likely to be diagnosed with this type of ADHD. Inattentive ADHD was previously known as ADD (Attention Deficit Disorder.)

3. Combined Type ADHD

Children or adults have combined type ADHD when they display six or more hyperactive types and inattentive type ADHD symptoms.

1.3 Symptoms of ADHD

ADHD symptoms in kids and adolescents are well-defined. Nevertheless, ADHD is a complicated condition. You cannot just pick a few symptoms from a list and call it a diagnosis. Every youngster exhibits different ADHD symptoms at some point in their life. On the other hand, adulthood ADHD symptoms and signs can be difficult to detect.

Following are some major ADHD symptoms in children:

Signs of Inattention

In ADHD, half of the problem is attention. Children with ADHD may struggle to pay attention to you or a teacher. Lack of attention makes it hard for the children to listen, learn, or think. The main indications of inattentiveness include:

- Getting distracted or having a short-attention-span
- Losing things or being forgetful
- Being unable to listen to instructions or carry them out
- Struggling with careless mistakes
- Being unable to focus on time-consuming or monotonous tasks
- Having difficulty being organized
- Constantly changing the task
- Getting easily distracted

Signs of Impulsiveness and Hyperactivity

The main symptoms of hyperactivity are:

- Constantly fidgeting
- Not sitting still, especially in quiet or calm surroundings
- Excessive talking
- Excessive movement
- Interrupting conversations
- Not waiting for their turn
- Acting spontaneously, without thinking
- Having little sense of danger (or maybe no sense of danger at all)
- Being unable to focus on tasks

1.4 Clinical features of ADHD

ADHD is usually diagnosed in children by a child psychiatrist, pediatrician, or a competent mental health practitioner. The diagnosis of ADHD is assisted by a complete history of your child's behavior from caregivers and teachers, psycho-educational testing, and observation of the child's behavior. Because ADHD is a collection of symptoms, its diagnosis requires examining data from various sources, including psychological, physical, and neurological testing.

Age: ADHD symptoms typically appear before a child is six years old. Also, the diagnosis of ADHD in childhood often persists in adolescence and adulthood.

Sex: As per research, boys are more likely than girls to be diagnosed with ADHD. Girls have greater chances of having inattentive type ADHD symptoms only. Girls are less expected to engage in disruptive conduct that intensifies ADHD symptoms. This means that girls with ADHD are not always diagnosed.

ADHD symptoms can occur in various settings, including at home or school. Children with ADHD have a pattern of inattention and hyperactivity-impulsivity that affects their ability to function and develop. Children may show signs of both impulsiveness and inattention, or they may show signs of only one of these behaviors. We have already seen some major signs of hyperactivity, impulsiveness, and inattention in the previous section.

Inattention

There is the likeliness of existence of inattentive ADHD type if:

- Six or more symptoms of inattention are present in children under the age of 16, or
- Five or more symptoms of inattention are present in adolescents and adults aged 17 years and older, and
- Symptoms of inattentiveness have been present for at least six months, and they are inappropriate for the developmental level.

Hyperactivity and Impulsivity

There is the likeliness of existence of Hyperactivity and Impulsivity ADHD type if:

- Six or more symptoms of hyperactivity-impulsivity are displayed in children under the age of 16, or
- Five or more symptoms are present in adolescents and adults aged 17 years and older; and
- Symptoms of hyperactivity-impulsivity have been displayed for at least six months and are disruptive and inappropriate for the person's developmental level.

Some other clinical features of ADHD in children may include:

- Emotional immaturity
- Procrastination
- Having significant sleep disturbances
- Distraction

Some children may also display signs of other related disorders alongside ADHD, such as:

- Anxiety
- Depression
- Autistic Spectrum Disorder (ASD)
- Dyspraxia
- Epilepsy

By now, we have learned about the types, symptoms, and clinical diagnosis of ADHD in children. In chapter 2, we will learn about the likely causes of this condition. We will also see the strengths associated with ADHD children.

Chapter 2: What You Should Know About ADHD

"My child is 17 already, yet he has poor decision making ability. He is left behind. I'm afraid what the future holds for him."

"My daughter's thoughts are not composed. There are huge barriers between her and the outside world. Only God knows how she'll catch up with the rest of the world."

"My son has severe behavioral issues. He is always depressed and anxious. I am afraid he is gradually moving towards substance abuse and self-injury. He is still so young; how will he spend his entire life this way?"

If you have an ADHD child, you might be well aware of the above-mentioned concerns.

Children with ADHD may face various challenges. Their thoughts may be jumbled up. Their focus may easily shift from one topic to another. Consequently, we may be quick to draw negative conclusions about their potential.

However, as parents or caregivers, we need to realize that ADHD is not the end of the world. We often place our entire focus on the negative aspects of ADHD and miss out on the positive ones. ADHD has many negative connotations because people misinterpret it. Children with ADHD are stereotyped as being lazy, less hardworking, and less smart. Therefore, such children are usually the victims of criticism or ridicule. Many people even wonder if ADHD children can achieve anything at all in their lives.

The truth is that various adults with ADHD have received the necessary treatment and care. They have learned to live without allowing ADHD disorder to control them. Yes, there are some positive aspects of having ADHD.

2.1 Positives of ADHD

Children with ADHD may possess incredible strengths, like being more optimistic and creative than others. Such abilities allow them to excel in various fields. In fact, some people define ADHD-related abilities as "ADHD superpowers" because a neurotypical child (not having ADHD) often lacks such skills. Therefore, if your child has ADHD, you do not need to be discouraged or allow the condition's drawbacks to overshadow its many potential benefits.

Some advantages of ADHD are mentioned below:

Creativity

Children with ADHD are usually highly creative, particularly when it comes to goal-oriented tasks. They approach tasks differently, which allows them to become effective problem solvers. Children with ADHD come up with novel solutions because of their unique perspectives. They are inventive thinkers. Some better words to describe such children may be creative, artistic, and original.

Intelligence

An ADHD child may have average intelligence. However, they may also have above-average intelligence levels. Unfortunately, many parents ignore their child's intelligence because they focus on poor grades, missing assignments, and behavior issues. Parents should realize that ADHD children have unique brains which may not be made for a traditional classroom environment. It is important to find your child's distinctive intellectual abilities and use such abilities to promote their learning.

Courage and Spontaneity

The impulsive nature of ADHD children leads to spontaneous events that produce lasting and enjoyable memories. Children with ADHD are not hesitant to do what they want. They do not worry about or overthink the long-term consequences of their actions. Consequently, children having ADHD are more likely to seek thrills and adventure, which gives them more courage.

Resilience

Children with ADHD may face setbacks and hardships which need to be overcome. Such children can develop resilience since they have experienced and overcome these challenges more frequently than others. Overcoming obstacles and developing resilience can result in a strong personality.

Studies have also highlighted that people with ADHD have greater self-awareness.

High Energy

Hyperactivity is one of the major symptoms of ADHD. Many people associate hyperactivity with an interruption in work. Nevertheless, hyperactivity also implies that individuals with ADHD excel at various physical activities, especially sports. Children with ADHD have the strength to flourish in an environment that promotes and rewards movement and exercise. So, hyperactivity can have positive effects on a child's life.

Hyper-Focus

Hyper-focusing is a condition in which a person with ADHD can concentrate on an activity for hours, effectively tuning out everything else. Hyper-focusing normally occurs when a person is engaged in a work that they find interesting and enjoyable.

While hyper-focusing, a child's performance can improve, allowing them to work more efficiently. This method permits them to accomplish a task without being distracted, and the result is often of high quality.

Conversational Skills and Empathy

Children with Inattentive ADHD Type are usually great conversationalists. They can bring up an intriguing conversation in different scenarios because they are talkative.

Such children also have a good sense of humor, empathy, and higher social intelligence.

2.2 Don't Let ADHD be a Hindrance to Success

Have you forgotten about your strengths as an ADHD individual? You should not underestimate your visionary imaginations. Your capacity to dream and hope is immense. Do you know why you stand out from the crowd?

As an ADHD individual, you:

- Have big thoughts and dreams.
- Can turn the smallest opportunities into major breakthroughs, all with the power of your imagination.
- Turn your dream into a living reality.

Today, many individuals with ADHD are leading successful lives with incredible careers. Various famous personalities with ADHD did not let ADHD be an obstacle to their success.

For example:

Michael Phelps is a former American competitive swimmer. He holds 28 Olympic medals (23 are gold.) The beginning was not easy for Phelps. His ADHD was diagnosed when he was 9. He struggled with school work as a child. Phelps' teachers would treat him differently than other kids in the class. One of the teachers told him that he would not be successful in life.

But Michael Phelps discovered his potential in swimming and is known by the world today.

Simone Biles, another medal-winning Olympic gymnast, has ADHD. Various award-winning singers, multifaceted actors, political analysts, commentators, and some popular television personalities have made great breakthroughs despite their ADHD symptoms. Adam Levine, Justin Timberlake, and James Carville are a few of them.

One common thing in all of the names mentioned above is that they did not give up. These celebrities show that a medical condition does not have to prevent you from leading a full and happy life. These well-known celebrities and various other less-famous people have discovered ways to succeed despite their ADHD.

The key is to find a suitable treatment plan for ADHD and follow it regularly. Early diagnosis of ADHD and a good treatment plan can help your child manage their ADHD symptoms. As per research, the multimodal approach is one of the best ways to manage ADHD symptoms in a child. The multimodal approach means using multiple methods of ADHD treatment together.

Multiple ADHD treatment plans are given below. We will look at some of them in more detail in the later chapters of this book.

1. Medication: Stimulants are commonly prescribed for ADHD treatment. They help to enhance attention span and control hyperactivity and impulsive behavior. However, individuals aged above six may take non-stimulants because the stimulant medications may not work for everyone. Sometimes, doctors may also prescribe antidepressant drugs for better results.

2. Therapy: Therapies primarily focus on behavior change. Therapy has various forms, such as:

- Behavioral Therapy
- Individual Therapy
- Group Therapy
- Family Therapy

3. Natural Remedies: Maintaining a healthy diet, exercise, and sleeping habits can help individuals with ADHD effectively manage symptoms. Some other natural remedies include light therapy. Light therapy may include an individual's exposure to natural sunlight or indoor artificial light. We will look at these remedies in more detail in Chapter 5 of this book.

4. Educating Parents: Parents' education about ADHD symptoms and their management is vital for treating ADHD.

5. Special Education: It helps a child with ADHD learn in a school environment. Such education brings an effective structure and routine to help ADHD kids.

2.3 Causes of ADHD

Research has shown that a combination of the following factors may be responsible for ADHD.

- **Genetics:** ADHD usually runs in families. It is assumed that the genes you acquire from your parents have a key role in developing the disorder. There is a one-in-four chance that an ADHD child might have an ADHD parent. According to research, siblings and parents of ADHD kids are more likely to have the disorder themselves. However, the inheritance of ADHD is assumed to be complicated and is not believed to be linked to any one particular genetic fault.

- **Brain Structure and Function:** According to research, the brains of ADHD individuals may be different from the brains of people without ADHD. For instance, studies including brain scans have revealed that certain parts of the brain in individuals having ADHD are smaller while other parts are larger. Other research has indicated that ADHD individuals may have imbalanced neurotransmitter levels in their brains. It is also possible that such chemicals (neurotransmitters) in the brain may not function properly. ADHD may be linked to reduced activity levels in those areas of the brain that deal with attention and activity level.

- **Prematurity:** Premature babies (born before the 37th week of pregnancy) or those with low birth weights are more prone to develop ADHD symptoms.

- **Brain Damage:** Brain damage may occur in a mother's womb or in the later part of life due to some severe head injury. In either case, brain damage leads to a greater risk of ADHD.

- **Epilepsy:** Children with epilepsy may face the risk of ADHD.

- **Prenatal Exposures:** Use of alcohol or intake of nicotine from smoking during pregnancy increases the risk of ADHD development in a newborn.

- **Environmental Risks:** A child's ADHD symptoms also depend on their environment. Exposure to environmental toxins at a young age or even during pregnancy raises the chances of ADHD. Lead is an example of an environmental toxin.

The known cause of ADHD may help parents deal with their child's symptoms in a better way. Also, there are various triggers, such as certain foods, poor sleep, stress, technology, and overstimulation, which may worsen your child's ADHD symptoms. Therefore, it is important to recognize such triggers and make important lifestyle changes to control your child's ADHD episodes.

In the upcoming chapter, we will focus on how ADHD in children can affect their families and siblings.

Chapter 3: Understanding ADHD for Parents

The symptoms that an ADHD child displays can range from moderate to severe. Such symptoms can be difficult to control. Consequently, having an ADHD child can cause significant stress in families, resulting in marital issues, greater conflict, or even increased rates of depression and divorce.

"Mother! You simply don't care about me anymore. All that matters to you is Emma. You didn't attend my school's meeting because you were with Emma. You have started ignoring me ever since Emma came. I know she is more important to you than me."

The above scenario depicts Sarah's frustration. Sarah is a 14 years old teenage girl whose younger sister, Emma, has ADHD. Emma was diagnosed with ADHD only when she was 4. Her mother's center of attention is Emma, and because of this, Sarah feels overlooked.

It is easy to forget about the siblings of ADHD children, yet they are also affected. The siblings of a child with ADHD are frequently overlooked or disregarded since their ADHD sibling appears to be the priority. Some children even feel responsible or guilty for their sibling's diagnosis, as if they caused it. As a result of feeling neglected, siblings may display anger, anxiety, embarrassment, and indulge in attention-seeking behavior.

You need to understand that your child's condition can affect your entire family. You also need to learn about the challenging behaviors associated with your child's ADHD symptoms and know how you can deal with the intense emotions. The upcoming sub-sections of this chapter will give you more insights into the matter.

3.1 How ADHD Affects Families

When a child has ADHD, it can cause disruptions in relationships and routines. Such disruptions affect not just the individual with the disorder but also the entire family. According to studies, having ADHD in the family might affect the quality of life of siblings, parents, and other family members.

For instance, children with ADHD place significantly more demands on their parents regarding their time and attention. Families with children who have ADHD face a higher number of developmental, behavioral, and educational issues. Such a situation often demands additional time, resources, and efforts from the parents. It can also lead to marital issues, a lack of family unity, and increased conflicts.

According to studies, parents of children with ADHD have higher divorce rates and depression than normal families. Both children and adults are at risk of mental and physical health problems when family situations are chronically stressed. The marital issue is common in ADHD families, and it has been persistently associated with negative health and mental conditions. Some people believe that marital issues have a damaging effect on a child because they:

- Reduce a child's sense of security and safety in their home.
- Upset parent-child relation.
- Bring an inconsistency in the discipline.
- Reduce parental supervision of potentially harmful behaviors.
- Promote aggressive behaviors.

Families can also face a great financial burden in treating their child's ADHD and related disorders. Parents may have to spend extra amounts on special child care institutes, medications, therapists, and an ADHD-specific diet. Also, parents or caregivers of ADHD children may have to be late for work or take more days off. Some parents even alter their employment status because of their child's need for greater attention. Such scenarios decrease parents' productivity at work and may lead to greater financial issues for the families.

3.2 Challenging Behaviour

Apart from difficulty paying attention, ADHD children have enormous behavioral issues too. When ADHD kids are told to do something they do not want to do, they may be stubborn, throw a tantrum or lash out. Although tantrums and stubbornness are not indicators of ADHD, they are usually associated with it. Children with ADHD may become frustrated. Impulsivity may force them to act up, for instance, tossing a shoe, pushing someone, or yelling at them. They are less capable of dealing with strong emotions without overreacting than other children of their age.

However, behavioral issues in ADHD children can be more than impulsive tantrums. Negative behavior patterns develop in some children with ADHD due to years of being in conflict with their parents or caregivers. Oppositional Defiant Disorder (ODD) is a behavioral condition identified in children with ADHD who are habitually rebellious.
ADHD children are more likely to be drawn to activities their parents do not want them to do. Such a situation can lead to conflict between ADHD children and their parents at an early age.

Discipline tactics that work well for other kids may be unhelpful for an ADHD child who has developed a habit of negative interaction. Losing your temper with an ADHD child will not work. Parents who raise their voices may impact a youngster who rarely misbehaves. However, children who are habitual of misbehaving may become accustomed to their parents' anger. If a parent yells frequently, such children will gradually accept it as the norm. Why should they pay attention when people would only yell at them? Similarly, punishment also loses its effectiveness for most ADHD children.

Children with ADHD often require more structure than other children. They also need clearer instructions about the behavior that an adult expects from them. Appreciation and providing opportunities for a pleasant relationship with parents are effective ways of managing the disruptive conduct of an ADHD child.

3.3 Dealing with 'Big Feelings'

Imagine you hear your 11-year-old shouting at her brother. She then comes running to you and screams about what her younger brother has done. It turns out that he only commented, "Your hair is super curly!" Your 11-year-old requires you to punish him for that comment and gets infuriated when you do not react. All night long, she keeps complaining about how unfair that was.

Do you think the child's reaction to this potential scenario is intense?

The majority of children with ADHD experience the same feelings as their peers. They experience the same emotions as everyone else: anger, hurt, sadness, worry, discouragement, and laziness. However, for many children with ADHD, these emotions appear to be more intense and frequent. Also, such emotions may be long-lasting and adversely affect everyday life.

ADHD children who struggle to manage their emotions can manifest them differently. As compared to other kids, ADHD children are more likely to:

- Worry excessively or for a long time about little matters.
- Have a hard time cooling down when angry.

- Feel hurt or offended by even gentle criticism.
- Get irritated by minor annoyances.
- Feel a strong desire to attain something they want right away.

Most children without ADHD can get over their emotions after a while. For instance, if they are discouraged, they may be able to tell themselves, "That's alright. I can try again or find a better way next time." If they are angry, they may tell themselves, "Chill out! It's not such a big deal." But ADHD children get caught up in whatever they feel at any moment. Their feeling in the "present moment" dominates all of their thoughts.

Moreover, it is important to note that most individuals with ADHD are extremely sensitive to what others say or think about them. This is commonly referred to as Rejection Sensitive Dysphoria (RSD). RSD is a term used to describe specific symptoms linked with ADHD. However, RSD is not a medical diagnosis. "Dysphoria" is derived from a Greek word that means "hard to endure." People with RSD have a hard time dealing with rejection. They become enraged if they believe they have been rejected or criticized, even if this is not true. Up to 99 percent of ADHD teenagers and adults are more sensitive to rejection than the general population. And nearly one-third of those with ADHD say dealing with "big emotions" is the most difficult aspect of their condition.

3.4 Effects on Other Siblings

ADHD has a major effect on siblings of children with the disorder. According to one study, ten of the thirteen siblings (who were interviewed) were "severely and unfavorably" impacted by having an ADHD sibling. Siblings stated that the disruption created by the behavior of ADHD children was the major difficulty faced by them. Examples of disruptive behavior included:

- Out-of-control hyperactivity
- Physical and verbal violence
- Social and emotional immaturity
- Learning challenges and academic underachievement
- Family conflicts
- Bad peer relationships
- Problematic interactions with extended family

According to the siblings (who were interviewed), family life was "exhausting," "chaotic," and "centered on their ADHD sibling." Siblings stated that the effect of ADHD on their lives would continue indefinitely.

As per the survey, siblings of ADHD children were affected by the disorder in three ways:

1. Being responsible for caring for their ADHD sibling
2. Being victimized
3. Feeling sadness and loss

Siblings defined victimization as verbal aggression, physical violence, and controlling and manipulative behavior. Many siblings felt that they were unprotected by their parents because the parents were thought to be too tired or overwhelmed to care for them.

Siblings stated that their parents expected them to act as caregivers for their ADHD sister or brother. Parents expected the older and younger siblings to supervise and play with their ADHD siblings. According to siblings, some examples of caretaking duties included:

- Giving medication
- Assisting with homework
- Speaking to other children and teachers on behalf of their ADHD sibling
- Keeping the ADHD child "out of trouble."
- Keeping the child engaged when the parents were exhausted

While some siblings expressed pride in their ability to fulfill this role, most said it was difficult, especially when they felt victimized by their ADHD sibling. Some individuals said they helped their parents but did not get much in return.

Siblings of ADHD children desired "peace" and "normal" home life. They were concerned that their ADHD brother would be hurt or go into trouble. Siblings believed that their parents wanted them to be self-sufficient. Because their needs appeared to be less important than those of their ADHD sibling, these youngsters usually felt forgotten or overlooked.

They stated that they tried not to add to their parents' burden.

Many siblings who were interviewed thought that their ADHD sibling controlled their family life. They believed that their ADHD brother or sister "ruined" all the enjoyable moments for them. A vast majority of such siblings (those interviewed) felt unworthy of their parent's love, care and attention.

Can you link the above-mentioned study with Sarah's example that we just read at the beginning of this chapter? Do you think that Sarah's frustration was justified? Parenting stress can be minimized, and family relationships can be enhanced by including parent training in ADHD management.

Chapter 4: Disorders Associated with ADHD

Various reports state that more than 60% of ADHD children have one or more mental health condition that co-exists with ADHD. The symptoms of co-existing mental health conditions often overlap with ADHD's symptoms, leading to a risk of misdiagnosis of ADHD in a patient. Misdiagnosis or a delay in diagnosis could be a major concern that may adversely affect the patient's mental health and quality of life.

Some of the major disorders in ADHD children are anxiety, depression, anger, and mood disorders. Such children may also face learning issues such as difficulty reading or making calculations. ADHD can also worsen sleep problems in children. Research suggests that children with ADHD are at risk of early cigarette use, followed by illegal drug and alcohol abuse.

Disruptive behavior disorders are commonly related to ADHD. Oppositional Defiant Disorder (ODD) and Conduct Disorder (CD) are examples of disruptive behavior disorders. Individuals with ODD have a pattern of losing their temper, arguing, blaming and deliberately annoying others, refusing to follow the rules and being vindictive, spiteful, and angry towards others. Similarly, children with Conduct Disorder (CD) may show aggression toward people and animals, lie or steal things, destroy property, skip school or even run away.

Another disorder is Tics and Tourette syndrome. Tics may involve sudden, involuntary, rapid, and recurrent vocalizations or movements. Examples of tics include eye darting, nose twitching, or throat clearing. If tics are complicated, they may even include repeating different words or phrases, stepping or hopping in a certain manner, or gesturing in a particular way.

On the other hand, Tourette is much rarer but more severe than tics. A patient with Tourette syndrome may yell a word or sound, make various noises, or repetitively flinch or blink their eye on a regular basis.

Usually, when a child has ADHD and other related conditions, the health care expert may decide to treat ADHD first. That is because basic ADHD treatment may improve the child's ability to deal with other conditions. We will look at ADHD treatment options in the upcoming chapters. Meanwhile, let us discuss the common disorders linked to ADHD in greater detail and the possibility of any misdiagnosis.

4.1 Misdiagnosis of ADHD

"I'm concerned that my 7-year-old has been misdiagnosed with ADHD. How can I be sure about that? And what can I do next?"

Do you have the same concern? If so, it is important to pay heed to such a matter and get more information about it.

If you are doubtful about your child's diagnosis, the first step is to get in touch with the expert who made the diagnosis. It is alright to inquire about an expert's medical background. The two primary areas you will want to inquire about are:

- The information based on which diagnosis has been made
- The way your child has responded to ADHD therapy

Inquire about the doctor's diagnosing procedure by asking if they:

- Were well-informed about your child's development. For a precise diagnosis, it is important to know when your child met developmental milestones in behavior and emotional regulation.

- Have asked you and your child's teachers to complete rating scales. The rating scales assist the clinician in making a diagnosis based on measurable data.

- Have gathered enough information about how long the child has been suffering from specific symptoms.

A child must have had various symptoms for at least six months to be diagnosed as an ADHD individual. These symptoms must also impact your child's capacity to perform in multiple environments. For instance, is your child regularly dealing with ADHD symptoms in school and at home?

When it comes to symptoms, another important question to ask is:

"How certain the clinician is that your child is suffering from ADHD and not some other issue?"

ADHD is often associated with several issues. However, such issues can also occur individually, leading to a misdiagnosis of ADHD.

The following factors may affect the credibility of a child's ADHD diagnosis:

Depression: Depressed children generally lack energy and are uninterested in social situations. However, children with ADHD may suffer mood swings and have difficulty getting along with their peers, but they still want to socialize.

Anxiety: ADHD and anxiety may look alike. Children with ADHD and anxiety may appear to be preoccupied or tuned out. However, the reasons for such behavior may be different in both cases. For instance, ADHD children struggle to be attentive because they have focusing issues. However, children with anxiety struggle to pay attention because they may be distracted by their fears or worries.

Sleep Problems: While ADHD can impair sleep, sleeping disorders such as sleep apnea can cause children to act in ways that resemble ADHD. Did the doctor inquire about specific aspects, such as whether your child wakes up frequently or snores loudly during the night? Such questions may help with the better diagnosis of underlying conditions.

Chronic Stress or Trauma: Trauma, such as neglect, abuse, or other childhood events, may result in ADHD-like behavior. On the other hand, chronic stress can be caused by a lack of support for ADHD and other problems.

Learning Differences: It might be hard to know why a child has difficulty in school. Is it due to a lack of concentration? Or is it because the child has difficulty reading? A child could also struggle with other skills required to do particular tasks. These learning issues may look similar to those in ADHD but may not be the same as ADHD.

Immaturity: According to studies, the youngest students in a class have more chances of being diagnosed with ADHD. It is possible that your child is just immature but has been mistaken as an ADHD kid. When the doctor and teachers examine your child's behavior, it is important to note if your child is among the youngest children in the class.

Interestingly, the issues mentioned above can also occur simultaneously with ADHD. It is usual for ADHD and other disorders to co-occur. Therefore, a proper ADHD evaluation cannot be done in a one-time appointment, lasting some 20 minutes. Is behavior therapy or ADHD medication not working for your child? That could be because your child does not have ADHD. On the other hand, there could also be a possibility that your child has not practiced the behavior therapy for long enough, so it is not working for them.

You can get a comprehensive neuropsychological evaluation. Such evaluation may provide more prominent indications about ADHD and other disorders. Also, an effective way to get more information about your child's condition is to consult their teachers. The teachers spend more time with your child in a specific environment than you or the child's doctor do.

4.2 Anxiety

Stress-Based Anxiety

Anxiety is common in children with ADHD. Blurting out, interrupting, fidgeting, and forgetting things are some of the signs of ADHD that can be quite disruptive and cause stress in youngsters. For example, children who are often scolded for speaking out of turn in class are more likely to experience stress and have low self-esteem. Working memory, organizational and time-management skills are issues for many children with ADHD. Due to such struggles, it may not be easy to stick to regular routines and accomplish short and long-term objectives. Such a situation can lead to chronic stress in ADHD children. Chronic stress creates anxiety.

Emotions-Based Anxiety

Emotional management is another issue that ADHD children face. ADHD causes a rush of emotions in children, which can be hard to regulate at the moment. Such emotions can be positive or negative. However, if a child is overwhelmed with anxiety and begins to ruminate with worries, he may find it hard to make sense of his ideas and become trapped in a loop of anxious and negative thinking.

Anxiety (whether short-term or long-term) can manifest itself in various ways. The symptoms of anxiety may change according to age group. Here are various behaviors that may indicate anxiety in ADHD children:

- The child seems argumentative or irritable.
- There is sleep disturbance.
- The child refuses to go to school.
- Such children avoid people. They may retreat to the bedroom or some other private space.
- The child has extreme fears about various situations, such as being separated from their parents. They may also be afraid of specific things, such as dogs or insects.
- The child is concerned about the present or future. They worry that something bad will happen.
- ADHD children with anxiety may display behaviors such as skin picking, hair twirling, or other anxious behaviors.

4.3 Anger

Some children with ADHD have regular outbursts of anger. Such furiousness can make it difficult for a child to retain friendships or behave properly at school. Some common reasons for anger outbursts in ADHD children are:

Impulsivity

Impulsivity associated with ADHD means if your child is

angry, they will express it immediately. Impulsive aggression affects more than half of preadolescents with ADHD.

Emotional Sensitivity

Children with ADHD are often sensitive and emotional and have deep feelings. They have difficulty controlling their emotions. This may prompt such children to become angry easily.

Moodiness

Comorbid mood disorders are common in children with ADHD. Mood disorders can induce short-temperament in a child.

Frustration

Individuals get frustrated when they cannot achieve their goals. "Frustration tolerance" is the ability to manage one's frustration. Low frustration tolerance can force your child to become frustrated fast, leading to anger outbursts.

Low Self-Esteem

ADHD can make it tough for children to achieve academic goals and make friends. This creates feelings of isolation and poor self-esteem. Low self-esteem can make your child angry.

Side Effects of Medication

When ADHD children's stimulant medications wear off, they may suffer a challenging period marked by more tantrums and meltdowns.

Excess Energy

The restlessness and energy that comes with ADHD can be overwhelming at times, resulting in a child's angry emotions and violent outbursts.

4.4 Mood Disorders

ADHD children are most likely to experience the following mood disorders:

- Bipolar disorder
- Major Depressive Disorder (MDD)
- Dysthymic disorder

Bipolar disorder is an extreme psychiatric condition. It includes psychotic symptoms (hallucinations or delusions) and self-destructive behaviors like suicidal thoughts, self-harm, and substance abuse. A family history of ADHD, mood disorder, bipolar disorder, or substance abuse is common in children with bipolar disorder.

Extreme mood swings, explosive outbursts, and severe behavioral issues are common in ADHD and bipolar disorder children. Such children are frequently aggressive and impulsive. They experience sudden, prolonged outbursts that are triggered by trivial frustrations. Such children may have a history of anxiety. They may also have:

- High energy levels
- Racing thoughts
- Excessive talkativeness
- Inflated self-esteem
- Overly sexual behavior
- Physical and mental agitation
- Less need for sleep

Generally, a child with ADHD and bipolar disorder has poor social skills. A child's behavior is unpredictable, hostile, and defiant, due to which family connections are usually strained. Initially, the symptoms of bipolar disorder may occur at home. However, as the child grows older, such symptoms commonly appear in other contexts.

Major Depressive Disorder (MDD) is a more severe type of depression. In addition to some obvious features of clinical depression and dysthymic disorder, an ADHD child with MDD displays the following behaviors:

- Constant depression and irritability
- Lack of interest in daily activities
- Withdrawal from other people
- Crying on a daily basis and being highly self-critical
- Talks about dying
- Planning or carrying out a suicide attempt

The irritability in an ADHD child having Major Depressive Disorder may remain constant. There may not be any clear reason for irritability in such children. Research has shown that socioeconomic status and intactness of a family may have minimal or no effect on a child's development of MDD.

The dysthymic disorder has the characteristics of:

- Low-grade chronic depression
- A state of demoralization
- Persistent irritability
- Low self-esteem

A child must have a minimum of two of the following symptoms to be diagnosed with the dysthymic disorder:

- Low-self-esteem
- Feelings of hopelessness
- Overeating or poor appetite
- Fatigue or low energy
- Excessive sleeping or insomnia
- Poor concentration

A child must have displayed these symptoms for at least a year before being diagnosed with dysthymic disorder. Also, these symptoms must show to impair the social, academic, and other areas of the everyday functioning of your child's life.

4.5 Depression

ADHD children have higher chances of depression than those without ADHD. Moreover, ADHD appears first, and depression shows up later when a child becomes a teenager or an adult.

Why does depression co-appear with ADHD?

ADHD children have to face various challenges. Such challenges can create depression. Behavior issues and school problems can erode the self-esteem of such children. ADHD can also have a social impact on children. Their classmates might exclude or tease them, making them feel alienated and hopeless. Also, ADHD children may be "pre-wired" to be depressed. Some ADHD-based chemical differences in their brain may make them feel more depressed. If ADHD co-exists with anxiety and substance abuse, the risk of depression increases. Furthermore, the age of ADHD diagnosis, family history, and gender affect the likelihood of depression in ADHD children.

Depression symptoms in ADHD children include:

- Feeling extremely down, i.e., a low mood
- Talking about feeling suicidal, hopeless, or helpless
- Giving up interest in favorite tasks
- Withdrawing from close ones and friends
- Changes in eating or sleeping patterns
- Not wanting to do home-work
- Refusing to go to school

- Getting angry or irritated over minor things
- Difficulty to focus

Moreover, depression can make children's ADHD behaviors more extreme. They may become more disorganized and distracted. Also, such individuals are more likely to get depressed in winter than others. The shorter winter days make it hard for them to adopt a healthy sleep schedule.

ADHD children feel compelled to "act in the moment" because of their impulsive nature. That is why families of depressed children (especially teens) having ADHD need to be particularly vigilant if such children talk about suicide or self-harm. Such children are more likely to make a suicide attempt than their friends without ADHD. If so is the case, the family should take immediate steps to find help.

In chapter 2, we discussed that ADHD is not the end of the world. Various renowned personalities around the world have ADHD and related disorders. Therefore, progress is always possible with the right treatment. The next chapters of this book are all about the treatments and remedies for effective ADHD management. However, it all starts with the belief and willingness to move ahead in life.

Part II: Treatment Strategies and Managing Behaviour

Chapter 5: ADHD Therapies and Natural Remedies

As a parent, you can greatly influence your child's treatment. Evidence suggests that eating a good diet, exercising regularly, and making various other smart choices might help your child manage their ADHD symptoms. Therefore, your child can begin their ADHD treatment even at home.

A balanced treatment plan that includes nutritious meals, exercise and play, learning different coping strategies, and developing social skills will enhance your child's academic performance, strengthen their connections with others, and reduce stress and frustration for your child and your entire family.

Behavioral therapy has shown to be an effective treatment for ADHD children. It is especially helpful as a co-treatment for children on stimulant drugs and may even enable them to reduce the medication's dosage.

Behavior therapy aims to reinforce desired behaviors through praise and rewards. Also, behavior therapy reduces harmful behaviors by setting consequences and limits. On the other hand, ADHD medication can also be used as a treatment option. ADHD medication affects everyone differently. Some children see a significant improvement, while others see little or no improvement. The side effects of such medication vary from child to child. Finding the right prescription and dosage may take time because everyone reacts differently to medication. Also, ADHD medication is more helpful when used in conjunction with other treatments.

This chapter will look at family and behavioral therapies and other natural remedies to enable your child to cope with their ADHD symptoms.

5.1 Behavioural Therapy

Behavioral therapy can assist ADHD children in developing new and more positive behaviors to help manage their symptoms. Behavioral therapy aims to change undesirable behaviors into positive ones. It teaches ways to enhance problem areas such as focus, organization, and impulse control.

Some ADHD individuals find that behavioral therapy enables them to control their symptoms without medication effectively. Others use medication alongside behavioral therapy. Behavioral therapy does not affect actual ADHD symptoms. For instance, it will not affect how a child's ADHD brain functions. However, it can teach ADHD children skills that will help them achieve in school, home, and relationships.

How Does Behavioral Therapy Work?

Behavioral therapy for ADHD children involves the "whole family approach" in changing behavior. It aims to modify the child's actions. Behavioral therapy also addresses how a child's negative behaviors should be handled at home. In many circumstances, parents of ADHD children unintentionally reinforce negative behaviors in their children.

That is why behavioral therapy involves a therapist who meets with the child's family to help them develop a strategy or a plan. Such a plan assists the entire family in setting goals and modifying their behaviors. Therapy sessions provide children and their parents with the tools necessary to make positive changes.

Children learn skills and methods for dealing with things that might be difficult for them, such as:

- Homework completion
- Attending class
- Keeping their rooms tidy
- Finishing daily responsibilities

On the other hand, parents learn new ways to assist their ADHD child in succeeding. They also learn why some strategies are ineffective. The therapist introduces new tactics for rewarding positive behaviors and managing negative ones during behavioral therapy.

Usually, your child would meet the therapist every month. You will learn ways to help them achieve their objectives at home and in the classroom. You will also learn ways to control their anger and practice self-control. In the first appointment with the therapist, you will discuss which behaviors are the most difficult. The therapist will then assist you in developing a plan to address those behaviors.

The therapist's plan will include establishing a "system of rewards and consequences" at home. You will make a chart outlining the steps your child must take to achieve their objectives and obtain rewards. The chart will show your child what they need to do each day to meet their goals. When children perform their required tasks and get rewards, they should be complimented and encouraged. However, children should not be shamed or punished for not completing their expected tasks.

Is Behavioral Therapy Working for Your Child?

If behavioral therapy is proving to be helpful, your child will show the following signs:

- The child will have improved performance at school.
- Your child will struggle less with tasks they have always found difficult.
- The child will seem less frustrated and more confident.

However, if your child shows no signs of improvement, you may need to consult the therapist and devise some other strategy for the cause. It is important to realize that behavioral therapy is not a "fix" or "cure" for ADHD. Your child will still have ADHD symptoms at the completion of behavioral therapy. However, such therapy will help them excel in areas they previously found challenging. The skills children learn in behavioral therapy remain with them for the rest of their lives. That can positively influence their success and independence in life.

5.2 Family Therapy

Family therapy refers to psychological counseling that aims to help family members resolve conflicts and improve communication. This, in turn, creates a better and more peaceful home environment. Family therapy is usually provided by a licensed therapist, clinical social worker, or psychologist.

How Does Family Therapy Work?

The techniques used in family therapy may depend on various aspects, such as the specific needs of the family undergoing the therapy. These techniques aim to focus on:

- Improving collaboration and communication
- Improving emotional awareness
- Enabling people to accept things that are beyond their control
- Assisting people to cope with major family changes

Family therapy is usually short-term. However, it can last for a year or longer if the family's situation and needs require so. Although such therapy usually involves all the family members, it may also focus only on those members who are willing to participate in the treatment.

During the sessions, the therapists usually inquire about the situation that led the family to undertake the therapy. They also examine other factors leading to family issues, such as environmental stress and underlying mental health problems. Family therapies are of different types. Some of them are listed below:

Family Systems Therapy: This approach helps family members focus on the strengths of their relationships and combat mental health issues.

Functional Family Therapy: This short-term treatment aims to help young individuals against violent or risky behavior or substance abuse. It provides teenagers and their families with healthy solutions to build trust and respect for each other.

Narrative Family Therapy: This approach encourages each family member to explain their perspectives and experiences to other members. That way, family members can view each other's problems more objectively than just viewing the situation from their perceptions.

Psychoeducation: This type of family therapy helps family members better understand their mental health conditions. Family members can provide a cohesive support system for each other when they know more about self-help approaches, medications, and treatment options.

Supportive Family Therapy: This approach aims to create a safe environment where family members can openly express their feelings and get their family's support.
Some therapists may rely only on a specific type of family therapy. However, others may follow a more multimodal approach that involves a combination of various types of family therapies, depending on the family's needs.

Is Family Therapy Helpful for ADHD Children?

ADHD children usually struggle to catch up with other children of their age. They may feel left behind in self-management, time-management, organization, and impulse control. This situation further creates relationship difficulties for such children with their families. That is when family therapy comes as a savior.

Family therapy is an effective treatment for ADHD children. It teaches parents effective ways to reinforce ideal target behaviors in their children. Family therapy also enables them to overcome problematic behaviors. Since ADHD children need immediate feedback, therapists work with the parents to establish an effective feedback system at home.

Moreover, family therapy helps strengthen the bond between children and their parents. Parents can learn how to be more supportive of their child's condition with the help of family therapy. Parents develop the skills to help their children become more confident and self-accepting. When children are able to develop a strong sense of resilience through their parents' support, they can manage their ADHD in a better way.

Living with ADHD can be hard. Such hardship elevates when one cannot connect with their parents and family and suffers in silence. This may cause ADHD children to develop anxiety, depression, and other difficulties. Family therapy helps parents understand and connect with their children more effectively. Children can turn to their parents to discuss their needs and feelings instead of acting them out in the form of violent behaviors. Family therapy further helps parents teach executive functioning skills to their children.

5.3 ADHD - Diet Management

Healthy and nutritious food can significantly influence the lives of ADHD children. Your balanced eating habits would help your brain function in a better way and reduce the ADHD symptoms, such as lack of focus or restlessness.

ADHD Recommended Diet

The following foods may prove to be helpful for ADHD management:

1. Protein-Rich Foods

Protein-rich diet includes foods such as:

- Meat
- Eggs
- Cheese
- Beans
- Nuts
- Low-fat dairy products
- Soy

These foods can be taken in the morning or as after-school snacks. They may improve concentration and make ADHD medications more effective.

Protein-rich foods make neurotransmitters in the brain. Neurotransmitters are the brain's chemicals used for sending signals throughout the body. A protein diet also prevents hyperactivity by overcoming the spike in blood sugar. When protein-rich foods are eaten for breakfast, they help produce brain-awakening neurotransmitters.

2. Complex Carbohydrates

These foods include the fruits and vegetables such as:

Apples

Grapefruit

Kiwi

Pears

Tangerines

Oranges

Foods with more complex carbohydrates can help your child get a better sleep when taken in the evening. Also, combining complex carbohydrates having high fiber and low sugar content with protein-rich foods can assist your child in managing ADHD symptoms during the daytime.

Sugar intake should be reduced during ADHD. Eating simple-processed carbohydrates such as waffles or white bread may increase your sugar intake. That is because our bodies quickly digest the simple processed carbohydrates into glucose (sugar). For instance, if your child's breakfast consists of a waffle with syrup and a glass of juice, their blood sugar will rise quickly. Their body will then respond by producing various hormones and insulin to drive sugar levels down to low. Resultantly, stress hormones will be released. This would cause your ADHD child to be stressed-out and irritable quickly.

Therefore, trying foods high in complex carbohydrates, proteins, and fiber is more helpful. Such breakfasts and lunches include a glass of milk, oatmeal, or peanut butter with a piece of whole-grain bread. Such carbohydrates digest sugars more slowly because a combination of proteins, fibers, and fats results in sustained blood sugar release. As a result, your child would show improved concentration and behavior at home and school.

3. Omega-3 Fatty Acids

Omega-3 fatty acids can be found in:

- Salmon
- Tuna
- Other cold water white fish
- Canola oil
- Olive oil
- Brazil nuts
- Walnuts
- Omega-3 fatty acid supplements

Omega-3 can improve concentration, impulsivity, and hyperactivity. Omega-3s are "essential fats" that are vital for normal brain functioning. Essential fats are the ones that are not produced by our bodies themselves. Rather our bodies get such fats from the foods we consume.

Research indicates that ADHD children have lower levels of omega-3. Therefore, your child may have to take supplementary fish oil to gain high levels of omega-3. Also, various researches have shown that omega-3 reduced the ADHD symptoms in children after a few months of intake.

The supplements contain 2 main omega-3 fatty acids:

- Eicosapentaenoic acid (EPA)
- Docosahexaenoic acid (DHA)

Omega-3 products having more EPS and DHA are more beneficial for ADHD children. Younger children are recommended a total dosage of 700-1000 mg per day, while older children should take 1500-2000 mg. However, it is important to ask for your doctor's advice and prescription before such intake.

Omega-3 comes in liquid, capsule, and chewable forms. The chewable form of omega-3 may not contain sufficient fish oil. Therefore, giving your child the proper dosage may be costly and time-consuming. On the other hand, if your child is too young and cannot swallow the capsule, you can give them omega-3 in liquid form. You can mix the omega-3 liquid in various foods, preferably smoothies or fresh juices, such as orange juice.

4. Maintain Iron Levels

As per a study, the average iron level of ADHD children (measured as ferritin) may be lower than those without ADHD. Another study revealed that increasing iron levels improved children's ADHD symptoms.

A "normal blood count" does not imply that ferritin levels are normal. It will be helpful to ask your child's pediatrician to test their ferritin level. If their ferritin levels are low, i.e., below 35, consult your child's doctor and start them on iron supplements. Alternatively, increase your child's intake of iron-rich foods, such as:

- Lean red meat
- Chicken

- Turkey
- Beans
- Shellfish

5. Check Magnesium and Zinc Levels

Magnesium and Zinc may play an important role in managing your child's ADHD symptoms. They improve concentration, attention, and overall brain health. Consult your child's doctor and pediatrician to ensure that the child is not low on these minerals.

Foods to Avoid in ADHD

Caffeine: Small amounts of caffeine may help with ADHD symptoms. However, the side effects of caffeine may outweigh its benefits. Caffeine can worsen its side effects if your child is on ADHD medication.

Sugar: Sugary foods may make your child more hyperactive. Therefore, sugar-rich foods should only be a small portion of your child's diet. You can try cutting such foods to see if the child's symptoms improve.

Food Additives: Food preservatives and artificial food coloring can worsen a child's ADHD symptoms. They may make children more hyperactive. However, the effects may vary according to the child's age and the type of additive being used. Various experts recommend that ADHD individuals should avoid the following:

- Artificial food colors, especially yellow and red

- Food additives such as nitrates, MSG (monosodium glutamate), and aspartame

Typical examples of foods with food additives and artificial colors are:

- Colorful cereals
- Soft drinks
- Packaged fruit punches
- Snacks such as candies and crisps

In some countries, the food regulatory authorities require warning labels on food packaging having artificial colors and additives. It is important to read food ingredient labels while looking for additive-free foods. Mostly, fresh and unprocessed foods have low additives.

Simple carbohydrates: ADHD individuals should avoid the following food items:

- White rice
- White flour products
- Sugar
- Corn syrup
- Candy
- Honey
- Skinless or peeled potatoes

Sensitive Foods: Research indicates that many ADHD children may be sensitive to various foods, making their ADHD symptoms worse. It might be possible that your child does not have any "medical food allergies" but he may still show worse symptoms when exposed to certain foods. A good way to learn about your child's food sensitivity to a certain food is to remove it from their daily consumption. If the results are favorable, avoid such food and consult a professional to follow the restrictive plan. Sometimes your child may show food sensitivity in allergic reactions such as eczema, asthma, or hay fever.

5.4 ADHD - Natural Remedies

The following natural remedies may prove to be helpful for ADHD.

1. Regular Exercise

Some helpful exercises for better learning for ADHD children are aerobics, sprints, and jumping jacks. There may be various other sports and exercises that could assist your child cope with their ADHD. Following are some great benefits of exercises and sports for ADHD children:

- Exercise is linked to an increase in neurotransmitters in the brain, particularly those in which many ADHD children are thought to be deficient. Exercise also boosts the quantity of brain-derived neurotrophic factors (BDNF), which is essential for learning.

- Overall, exercise is a vital aspect of a healthy lifestyle. It is important for your child's optimal performance. Sleep issues are frequent in ADHD children. According to one study, physical activity can assist individuals with ADHD cope with sleep problems.
- Exercise can train your brain for learning. Research indicated that after 20 minutes of aerobic activity, ADHD children improved their math and reading skills. Another research revealed that 30 minutes of physical exercise before school enhanced moodiness and overall ADHD symptoms in children.
- Sports can boost your child's self-esteem and motivate them to achieve their goals. Team sports, in particular, are linked to improved executive function in youngsters because they require higher cognitive engagement.

Encourage your children to exercise after school. Allow them to walk or ride their bikes home (if safe). Set a schedule for 30 minutes of physical exercise after your child arrives home from school. Engage them in exercise before they begin homework or other indoor activities. To boost your child's motivation, make sure to praise them afterward.

After-school swim lessons, karate class, and soccer practice are excellent sports options. Leisure time spent running around the park is also effective. On the other hand, you can inquire about your child's gym lessons and motivate them to learn the new skills.

Moreover, children's executive functions have been connected to traditional martial arts, notably Taekwondo, which emphasizes self-control and character development.

2. Exposure to Green Space

Researchers believe that more exposure to green space and nature may lower the risk of developing ADHD.

Researchers linked ADHD diagnoses with residence locations among people in Denmark. They tracked children's exposure to green areas from birth to age five. Researchers discovered that children living in locations with the minimal possible vegetation (such as parks, trees, and yards) had a higher likelihood of developing ADHD from 5 and up. ADHD was lowest in those children who had the highest accessibility to green spaces.

There are various reasons why greater exposure to green space can benefit the brain health of ADHD individuals.

- Less air pollution
- Less noise
- More social interaction
- More physical activity
- Fewer stress levels
- More microbial diversity in the gut
- Stronger immune system
- Improves sleep
- Improved focus and concentration
- Lower risk of anxiety and depression

Because of these benefits, green areas have also been known to reduce symptoms of "inattention."

Green spaces can also provide some escape from potentially over-stimulating activities. Being outdoor has the advantage of preventing children from looking at their smartphone screens. Getting away from modern devices allows kids to engage in more slow-paced activities in nature. And the slower-paced activities can have a calming effect on children, which helps reduce ADHD symptoms. For instance, listening to the chirping birds and gazing at flowers is more relaxing than playing a fast-paced, loud video game.

3. Herbal Treatment

The following herbal treatment options may effectively manage your child's ADHD.

Herbal Teas: Herbal teas containing lemongrass, spearmint, chamomile, and other flowers and herbs may be safe options for ADHD children who want to relax. Herbal teas help with better rest and sleep. These teas are recommended to be used before bedtime.

Pine Bark Extract: Proanthocyanidins are natural compounds found in pine bark extract. Research has shown that the extract made from such compounds lowers hyperactivity and increases concentration and attention. Another study indicated that providing the extract to youngsters with ADHD helped regulate antioxidant levels for a month. According to one study, a natural compound found in pine bark extract reduces stress hormones by 26%. It also reduces neuro-stimulant dopamine levels in ADHD individuals by roughly 11%.

Green Oats: These are the unripe oats, also known as Avena Sativa. The wild oat extract is taken from the immature crop. Green oats help relieve anxiety and stress and calm the nerves. Studies show that green oats may enhance concentration and attention, reducing ADHD symptoms.

Ginseng: Ginseng is a herbal remedy. It has been used in China for centuries. Ginseng is known to boost energy and stimulate brain function. The "red ginseng" variety is particularly helpful for reducing ADHD symptoms.

The research was conducted on ADHD children aged 14-16 years. The research revealed that when researchers gave 1000 mg of this herb to children for about 8 weeks, there were improvements in children's social functioning, personality, and anxiety issues.

Gotu Kola: This herb naturally grows in South Pacific, South Africa, and Asia. It is rich in nutrients that are good for healthy brain function. Such nutrients include Vitamins B6, B1, and B2. Gotu Kola reduces anxiety and improves mental clarity, thereby improving ADHD symptoms. It is particularly helpful in enhancing the memory domain.

Brahmi: This herb is also called water hyssop. This wild marsh plant grows in India. The herb is extracted from the leaves and stems of the plant. Brahmi improves memory and brain functioning. It improves the ability to retain new information. Studies indicate that this herb reduces ADHD symptoms such as impulsivity, inattention, poor self-control, and restlessness.

Ginkgo Biloba: Ginkgo Biloba belongs to a tree species native to China. It has various health benefits. This herb enhances mental sharpness and brain function. It further reduces ADHD symptoms in individuals. However, Ginkgo Biloba may not be a good choice for those having bowel diseases.

4. Essential Oils

Essential oils refer to the plant extracts refined into concentrated forms. These extracts are taken from the plant's roots, stems, leaves, and blossoms. Essential oils have been used to enhance mental and physical health for a long time. Studies have shown that oils such as rosemary, vetiver, and lavender may help improve focus and sleep. They have calming and soothing properties that may help to reduce anxiety and stress. All such properties may help improve the ADHD symptoms in an individual.

5.5 Ways Your Child Can Fight Depression

Apart from taking medications and other ADHD treatments, changing lifestyle can help alleviate the depression that co-exists with ADHD. Your child can manage their depression in the following ways:

1. Getting More Sleep

Many individuals with ADHD have difficulty falling asleep. Sleep deprivation can exacerbate ADHD symptoms. Sleep deprivation decreases your child's ability to cope with everyday life matters and makes them depressed. Make sure your child goes to bed simultaneously every night to optimize their sleep habits. They should avoid sports, exercise, or other distracting activities for at least an hour before bed. Before going to bed, they should take a bath or hot shower. Consult a doctor if your child's sleep difficulties persist.

2. Exercising Regularly

A daily exercise helps your body release endorphins, which are natural mood enhancers. It makes falling asleep at night simpler, and more sleep equals better moods. Furthermore, if your child workouts outdoors, they will be exposed to sunshine, which is good for their mental health. Make sure your child takes a daily 30-minute stroll in a natural location for a great benefit.

3. Do Not Give in to Stress Too Quickly

Your child can become so wrapped up in their everyday activities that they can forget to take a step back and assess stressors. Make your child write down their feelings if stress affects their mood. Make them note the greatest concerns in their day. Then figure out how to minimize or eliminate them.

4. Increase Outdoor Time

According to recent studies, children with ADHD who spend more time in natural environments have less severe ADHD symptoms. Green time should be a minimum of 30 minutes per day. Increasing your child's green time boosts their exposure to sunlight, a fantastic mood enhancer. You can take your child on a bicycle ride, walk them to the nearest park, or plan a picnic together with them.

5. Cut Down On Carbohydrates

Your child can turn to high-carb snacks when they feel down, e.g., an ice cream, a candy bar, or crackers. These snacks might boost their moods in the short term. But later on, they gain weight, become more fatigued, and experience depression. It is better to stick with low-carb and protein-rich snacks such as nuts or fruits instead of starchy and sugary items.

6. Track Your Child's Progress

Making a progress chart can be beneficial. Make a monthly chart with 31 days and include exercise, sleep, nutrition, green time, sunshine, and stress categories. On a scale of one to ten, ask your child to rate their depression each day. Your child will earn a checkmark for each category in which they succeed:

- Daily exercise
- 30 minutes of green time
- 30 minutes of sunshine
- At least 7 hours of sleep
- Lower-stress day
- Low- carb diet

Tell your child to get at least three checks per day for the first month. Strive for four daily checks in the second month. Of course, the ultimate goal is to incorporate all of these mood-boosting activities into your child's everyday routine.

It is important to note that any strategy or remedy may work for one child but may not be helpful for the other. Therefore, it is important to consult your child's professional or expert before opting for any particular treatment plan, especially for an ADHD diet plan.

As parents, you need to accept your child's condition. Any support from your end will help boost your child's morale and better manage their symptoms.

Chapter 6: Management of Associated Disorders

Various disorders that co-exist with ADHD can make an affected child's symptoms worse. That is why it is important to manage not just the ADHD symptoms but also the conditions associated with ADHD. Controlling issues such as anxiety, depression, and self-discipline will help alleviate your child's ADHD symptoms.

Therefore, in this chapter, we will learn some helpful strategies to control various disorders related to ADHD effectively.

6.1 Managing Your Child's Depression and Anxiety

When children are persistently anxious, parents tend to protect their children from harm. But they can unintentionally exacerbate the child's worry. This usually happens when parents want to protect their children from their fears and insecurities. Here are some suggestions for assisting your ADHD child in overcoming depression and anxiety.

- Practice relaxation strategies with your child. You can teach them various deep breathing exercises to remain calm in any situation. Also, progressive muscle relaxation exercises can help when children feel tensed. The technique for such exercises is simple: tighten and hold specific muscle groups for 5 seconds and gradually release them. Your child will feel relieved all of a sudden.

- Find relaxation tools for your child. For example, you can transform the child's room into a light blue theme. Colors such as lighter shades of blue may help provide mental relaxation. Also, consider including coloring books, mini sandbox or clay, fidget toys, stuffed animals, or a soothing music in your child's relaxation tools.
- It might not be a practical approach to eliminate the situation that triggers your child's anxiety. For instance, if your child starts crying in a particular situation and is relieved when you come to their rescue, it might only be a short-term solution. However, when the situation arises again, your child will seek your help instead of dealing with the particular problem themselves. That will make your child increasingly dependent on you. Rather, help your child accept the existing situation and learn to deal with such circumstances that make them concerned.
- You cannot assure your child that their concerns are unrealistic. For example, they won't fail a test, or another child won't laugh at them during school. However, you can show them confidence that they will be fine and that they will be able to handle any particular situation. You can also assure them that their anxiety will decrease with time when they learn to face their fears. This would assure them that your expectations are reasonable and that you will not ask them to do something they are incapable of.

- Respect your child's anxious feelings, but do not empower them. For example, if your child is hesitant to go to the doctor because they are afraid of injection, tell them that their fear is valid. However, encourage them to get through the situation with a positive mindset and assure them everything will be alright eventually.
- Do not feed your child's anxiety by asking leading questions. For example, instead of asking them, "Are you anxious about the school's meeting?" ask them, "How do you feel about the school's meeting tomorrow?" Keep your questions more open-ended.
- Discuss your child's worse fears with them and try finding possible solutions together. Understand what your child is afraid of. Ask them the reason for being afraid of a particular situation. Then devise a plan to assure them that their fears would not come true. This may be a good approach to divert their mind toward positivity.
- Be patient with your child. Anxiety or depression is not something your child can get rid of overnight. You need to see things from their perspective. Do not try to force solutions onto them. Provide them with some time and space to understand things in a better manner.

6.2 Managing Your Child's Anger and Emotional Outbursts

If your child has emotional outbursts, and their anger interferes with their relationships and life quality, you should guide them on how to control their emotions effectively. A mental health professional can also be highly beneficial in this regard. Following are some anger management tips for your child:

- Help your child express their feelings through "words." When children cannot communicate or understand their feelings, they are more likely to be violent. A child who cannot verbalize "I am angry" may try to show their anger through violent outbursts. Similarly, a child who cannot perceive or express sorrow may misbehave to obtain your attention.
- Take a piece of paper and draw out an anger thermometer. Label the thermometer from 0 to 10. Show them what happens to them at different numbers on the thermometer scale. For example, denote 0 with a happy, smiley face, while 10 with an unpleasant red face. An anger thermometer will help your child recognize their anger. When they feel angry, they would relate their face to the angry red face on the thermometer and will sense the thermometer temperature rising. Eventually, they will attempt to cool down.
- Make a plan for your child to calm down. Teach your child what they should do when they are furious. When frustrated, they might go to their bedroom or a specified "calming area" at home rather than throwing tantrums or becoming violent. Encourage your child to read a book, color, or do some other calming activity until they feel better. Also, consider making a relaxation kit. This may include your child's favorite

crayons and coloring books, toys, stickers, a scented lotion, or a comic book to read.

When your child is angry, you may tell them, "Go to your calm-down area," or "Get your relaxation kit." This will enable your child to manage their anger.

- Help your child cultivate anger management tactics. For example, teach them to count to 10, take a quick walk, or repeat some helpful phrase to divert their minds.
- Do not give in to your child's tantrums. For example, if your child is throwing a tantrum for a toy, and you buy them the toy to calm them down, this will only be a short-term solution. But it will worsen the situation in the future. Your child will see tantrums as an effective way to get their demands fulfilled in the future. Instead of meeting your child's unnecessary needs to calm them down, a better approach is to teach them to work on their patience.
- If your child is exposed to violent content through video games or television shows, their anger situation will get worse. It will effectively expose them to shows, games, and books that teach them healthy conflict resolution skills.
- Teach the child self-discipline by exposing them to the consequences of anger. Give them polite indications that disrespectful behavior is not encouraged. For example, if the child breaks something when angry, include them in repairing the said item or have them do chores to raise the repair money.

6.3 Building Confidence Using a Reward System and Other Strategies

A reward system is a behavior modification and discipline development method that parents may employ to encourage their children to substitute positive behaviors for bad ones. Rather than punishing a youngster for misbehavior, they reward them for good behavior.

Positive reinforcement helps children enhance their behavior and make better choices. When a child receives positive reinforcement, praise, and rewards for making a good decision, they are more likely to repeat those behaviors rather than the negative ones.

Children's self-esteem and self-image can be improved by using reward systems. Praise and other positive reinforcers can help children learn to manage acceptable limits and expectations from their parents, which can help them create trust.

Here are some keys to a positive reward system:

- Select a preferred behavior or task (you want your child to learn.)
- Make realistic expectations.
- Involve your child in reward selection.
- Provide your child with clear guidance regarding the skill.
- Be patient while your child learns new skills.

- Encourage your child through praise and the promised reward when attempting to accomplish the given task. Follow through with your promises.

When a child is frequently rewarded for doing good work, they start believing in their capabilities. As a result, their confidence goes up.

Some other helpful tips for building confidence in your child are as follows:

- Be a good role model for your child. When your child sees you tackling difficulties optimistically, they will follow your example. As a result, they will be more confident in their abilities.
- Tell your child not to get upset over their failures and mistakes. Ensure them that mistakes are for better learning and improvement. Confident individuals do not let fear of failure get in their success.
- Encourage your child to try new things and diversify their skills. This would raise their capability to tackle any situation that comes their way. Ultimately, their confidence will increase.
- Let your child find their passion. When they know about their interests and priorities, they will develop a sense of identity. Also, encourage them to enlist their goals. Working towards their goals will help them realize their talents and boost their confidence.
- Make your child feel valued and connected by involving them in household activities and decision-making.

- Teach your child that seeking perfection is an unrealistic approach. Rather, encourage them to accept their uncontrollable aspects. Develop a sense of uniqueness in your child.

6.4 Tips to Develop Social Skills

The following tips may help develop good social skills in your child:

- Learn about your child's interests and encourage them to participate in relevant activities. For example, if they like a specific sport, help them join the club for that sport in their school or any other after-school club.
- Encourage your child to better connect with others by asking questions. Asking questions can initiate a conversation and help form connections. That way, your child may feel more social and overcome any introversion (if any.)
- Practice role-playing with your child. Make your child play the role of the individual with whom they are having trouble communicating or getting along. This will offer you an understanding of who this person is or how your youngster perceives them. Then switch roles to evaluate how your child behaves when acting as if they are interacting with the person with whom they have troubled relations. Suggest to your child how they can communicate more successfully with the individual. When advising your child, remember to

teach them body language cues such as smiling or making eye contact.

- Teach empathy to your child. When your child is aware of others' feelings, they can form positive bonds with them. Practice good listening skills with your child. Also, teach them to be careful of others' feelings and interests.
- Learn about your child's limits. Do not push your child to be outgoing if they have an introverted nature. Especially, ADHD children may have special needs and feel comfortable socializing only a few hours a day. Make them feel safe by responding to their needs instead of fitting them into social norms.

6.5 Strategies for Self-Discipline

Parents should take a different approach to self-discipline if their child has ADHD. A few easy adjustments to your parenting practices could provide your child with the tools to better manage their behavior. These self-discipline techniques can assist a child with troublesome behaviors follow the rules.

1. Give Positive Attention

It might be difficult to parent an ADHD child. Even the most patient parents can become exhausted by their child's never-ending stream of energy and desire to chat incessantly. Nevertheless, providing positive attention to a child with ADHD is a wise investment. Positive playtime minimizes the need for attention. It may also improve the effectiveness of your repercussions. Reserve one-on-one time with your child each day, no matter how tough their conduct has been. One of the easiest yet most effective strategies to address an ADHD child's behavior problems is providing 15 minutes of positive attention.

2. Give Clear and Effective Instructions

ADHD children may need extra help when it comes to following instructions. That is because they have a short attention span. While giving any instructions to your child, make sure you have their full attention. Turn off any background noise, such as a TV, and make proper eye contact with your child while requesting a task. Place a hand on their shoulder while talking to them. That will help you catch their attention. Then give them one task or instruction at a time instead of a chain of instructions. If you give your child multiple tasks at a time, they may forget them all or might not be able to focus. Also, ask your child to repeat what they heard to ensure they understood the things clearly.

3. Give Praises and Feedback

Praise your child's efforts frequently. That will help them with self-esteem and also improve their behavior. Frequent feedbacks are important for an ADHD child's discipline.

4. Practice Time-Out

Time-out means taking a break and retiring to a quiet place to practice calmness. When your child breaks the discipline, show them to a quiet area in your house and guide them to calm down. Make it a habit to practice calmness with your child. That would ultimately help them with their self-discipline.

5. Allow Natural Consequences

You may need to choose your battles wisely when disciplining an ADHD child. Sometimes, it may be helpful to let things be instead of forcing specific choices onto your child. For example, if your child is unwilling to leave playing activity to have lunch, do not try convincing your child to eat. When they are hungry later, they will have to wait for dinner. Consequently, they will be motivated to have meals on time when served.

6. Coordinate with Child's Teacher

When parents and teachers work together, it may help a child become more disciplined at home and school. For instance, parents and teachers can devise a behavior management plan and implement it simultaneously at home and school.

6.6 Academic Skills Development

The following tips may help enhance your child's academic performance and related skills:

- Designate a study area at home. Ensure that the study area is away from all distractions. You may set the area as per your child's needs or even ask the child to organize it.
- Work with your child to maintain a study planner. Write down all the key dates and deadlines on the planner. Also include the tasks, assignments, or home-

works to be done in the planner. Ask your child to checkmark the task that has been done.

- Keep the workload off your child by breaking large projects into smaller tasks. Make an effective plan to achieve those smaller tasks within an effective time.
- Help your child learn through animated visuals or some other interesting techniques. That would help them build clear concepts and overcome any cramming. Such techniques would also develop the child's attention and interest in studies and overcome procrastination.
- Teach your child to build effective working relationships at school so that they can seek help from friends and teachers if any concept is not clear. Tell your child not to hesitate to bring up questions for their teachers.

It is important to understand that ADHD children might have learning abilities different from their peers. They may need different study strategies compared to those used for other children. Therefore, parents need to understand their child's capacity and devise study plans accordingly. Eventually, whatever the results may be, do not forget to praise your child for their efforts. Patience is the key to leading your child to succeed. And parents' support is vital to helping ADHD children catch up with other individuals their age.

Conclusion

Now that you have finished reading this ADHD guide, we hope you have grabbed many important aspects of the topic. The most important part is the effective understanding and implementation of core remedies.

The symptoms that an ADHD child displays can range from moderate to severe. Such symptoms can be difficult to control if not dealt with correctly. 60% of ADHD children have one or more mental health condition that co-exist with ADHD. Some of the major disorders in ADHD children are anxiety, depression, anger, and mood disorders. ADHD affects not only the child in question but also the quality of life of siblings, parents, and other family members.

A balanced ADHD treatment plan includes healthy diet, exercises, learning different coping strategies, and social skills. The right treatment option will help improve your child's performance in various aspects such as academics and relationships. Your child will also be able to cope with stress and related issues.

Behavioral therapy can assist ADHD children in developing new and more positive behaviors to help manage their symptoms. It helps to change undesirable behaviors into positive ones. Likewise, family therapy assists the entire family in dealing with a child's condition.

Natural remedies such as more exposure to sunlight and green spaces have shown commendable results in managing a child's ADHD symptoms and mental well-being. Various herbs such as green oats and herbal teas can help with mental relaxation and effective brain functioning.

Parents can work with their children to manage their symptoms through rewards and praise. Parents should also coordinate with their teachers to help boost their trust, discipline, and academic performance.

ADHD Child's Handbook serves as a comprehensive guide to parents with ADHD children. It encourages them to deal with their child's condition effectively. We believe that the child's first step towards improvement begins with the parents' and caretakers' consistent support.